Table of Contents

I0468944

FOREWORD

The circumstances that caused me to write this book didn't have to happen.

The story I'm about to share with you is true, the names have been changed and other specific info has been changed, but this could happen to anyone.

Who am I? I'm Bill Black, a Certified Exit planner, I've been helping business owners to prepare and protect their businesses for the last 30 years. I'm also the Founder and Host of the Exit Coach Radio Show that airs on KLAA 830AM radio here in Los Angeles on Sundays, and my podcast of the same name plays worldwide on iTunes. And I'm an Author. Besides this book I have written "100 Words from 100 Advisors on Exit Planning for Business Owners", with excerpts from 100 of the over 1,000 interviews I have done with Advisors and Authors. (It's available on Amazon and Kindle.)

As a result of the situation I'm about to describe, I embarked on a mission to help motivate 1 million business owners to plan so their family would not be the "Victim of an Unplanned Business". That's right, I said "Victim". You will see why as you read through the story in the first Chapter. The good news is that with a little time and a relatively small amount of money you can make sure this story is not repeated in your household.

It is estimated that 85% of privately help businesses have done little to no planning in the area I am about to describe. Help me change that. Please share this story with others you know. Don't assume they have done the planning. Most likely, they haven't.

Note: The information contained in this book is for informational purposes only and should not be considered to be tax or legal advice. Always consult your tax and legal advisors before implementing planning steps such as those contained in this book.

Bill Black is a Registered Representative of and Securities offered through Crown Capital Advisors, LP, member FINRA/SIPC. Advisory services offered through HM Barth & Company, LLP, a registered investment advisor. CA Insurance license #0652621.

CHAPTER 1. THE GROWTH MINDSET

I'd like to introduce you to George and Pam. Imagine that you know them (you probably know someone just like them). They are both age 57, they have two kid ages 27 and 21, and they have owned and operated a construction business for the last 25 years. With a lot of hard work and determination, they've built it up to 60 employees with $7 million in Annual revenues and have 4 locations.

George has called a meeting and is all fired up today. He has been approached by a competitor up north and they would like to sell their business to George for a very reasonable price. The reason they want to sell is that the Owner of that business retired 3 years ago and he put his son in charge. The problem is that the son was not exactly, shall we say, "CEO material", and now the business is faltering.

In fact, it's very rare that a family business succeeds a management transition to a next generation. There is usually way too much taken for granted when a son or daughter comes in. Sometimes the father or mother handing the business off is just burned out and they need to get out and the son or daughter is the natural path and they assume that everything will be alright if they can just keep the business running and maintain the status quo.

Many times the son or daughter has new ideas they have been just itching to implement and when Mom or Dad is finally gone they go to work to implement those changes.

In this case, the Son of the owner did not possess the same "people skills" as the Dad and as a result the company had lost customers and burned bridges with a few vendors and revenues were down. The employee morale was also down because the company had not paid the "expected bonuses" they were used to receiving in a couple of years. Further, because employee morale was down sloppy work was being done and accidents had occurred, driving up work costs and the Worker's Compensation insurance costs.

But George saw beyond that. He saw the potential to expand his territory, cut costs, blend employees into his excellent culture and immediately reduce the Worker's Compensation costs. It was a path to double his business overnight and he was excited. The bank had initially been hesitant but they were coming around and George had told his Key Employee he would "cut him in" on the new opportunity, and that's what George wanted to talk about at the meeting.

So we talked about ways to help the Key Employee "feel like an owner" without actually giving him stock. We discussed "Phantom Stock" plan designs – in particular a version called a "Stock Appreciation Rights" plan design that gives employees a share of the growth of the company, but that ties in employees to the Company with a "vesting schedule" (which provides that employees who leave the company forfeit some or all of the benefit). We also talked about another version called a "Controlled Bonus Plan" that is immediately tax deductible to the company (like a cash bonus) but that is not accessible by the employee for a period of years (again, to retain the employee).

George was excited. We talked about growth and expansion and what that would mean for his family and his future.

But Pam was concerned. Near the end of the meeting she said "I don't know if you know this, but we haven't planned for a lot of the "basics". We don't have a Living Trust or Employment Agreements and I feel like we need to do a lot of work in those areas before we can grow or expand the business."

I was shocked. I had assumed that they were all taken care of in the basic planning areas. I said "I did not know that and I agree that it is critical that we get the "basics" in order quickly and we will discuss that first at our next meeting."

That was on March 1, 2015. I want you to remember that day. I know I always will.

CHAPTER 2. THE UNTHINKABLE

There is a business survey that purports that over 85% of US business owners have done little to no planning for business continuity and succession (2014 PriceWaterhouseCoopers small business survey).

Little to no planning.

On March 16th, two weeks after our first meeting, the unthinkable happened. It was a Sunday, and George and Pam started the day as they started most Sundays, drinking coffee while perusing the Sunday newspaper, enjoying each other's company and the break from the 6 days of hustle-bustle they endured each week. After an afternoon of running errands and tending to family matters, George headed to the gym for a workout.

While exercising on a treadmill, George had a heart attack. It came on quickly and by surprise and George was in motion when it happened. As he fell he hit his head hard. By the time the Paramedics got there George was in trouble. He was pronounced brain dead at the hospital.

The next morning, my phone rang, early. I was on my way to a breakfast meeting and I picked up the call on my speaker phone. Pam's voice was shaky. "He always said if anything happened to call you", she said. I knew immediately that something was horribly wrong. I pulled over.

"What happened?" I said. She told me what happened and that she was worried and didn't know what to do.

That afternoon, I went to the hospital. George was on life support, but only so that they could determine if he could be an organ donor and so that some out of town relatives could say goodbye. George was gone and was not coming back.

Before I left, I whispered in George's ear "Your death will not be in vain. I'll see to that."

Tearfully, Pam and I set up a meeting for the next day at her house.

CHAPTER 3. A WIDOW'S QUESTIONS

The day after George passed away, I met the family to find out where things were and to what extent we would need to do damage control. The questions Pam asked me were exactly what you would expect her to ask (and indicative of the fact that most Owners do not talk along the lines of planning, even with their spouses.)

She asked me questions like;

- ***"What should I do with the business?"*** Their son had been working in the business as a manager of an office and doing a great job, but was he ready to run the business? This can be a very awkward and difficult discussion, especially when emotions are running high.

- ***"Where will I get income?"*** George was the President, and earned the President's salary. But Pam didn't work in the business, and was not entitled to get the President's paycheck as a salary, even though she was the owner. And bills were due and the next paycheck was needed to pay them.

- ***"What do I need to do next?"*** The problem with owning a business is that it really doesn't care who's alive and who's not. It opens for business the next day, there are orders to process, jobs to do, fires to put out.

- ***"Who should I trust?"*** While George had told Pam to call me, I didn't know the CPA or who else should represent them for Legal issues, HR issues, Real Estate issues, etc. Over the next year I referred in over 20 Advisors for various needs.

All were questions I thought maybe they had talked about at some point in their relationship, but obviously not, because she was asking these questions now. And we knew George's intentions, but not his methods.

GEORGE'S KNOWN INTENTIONS

Pam said George's intentions were to

sell the business to the key employee,

and pay Pam a wage until the business

could be sold to the Employee.

CHAPTER 4. BAND-AIDS

The next day we met with the Key Employee, Al. We discussed George's intention to sell the business to him and asked if Al had any knowledge of a plan or had discussed this with George. He hadn't. And Al was quick to point out that he had no extra money for a down payment. How do we sell the business to the key employee if he has no money?

We started with meeting with the CPA to discuss selling the business to the key employee. The key employee made a lowball offer, because he felt that he had helped grow the business so he should get a steep discount. We agreed that the value of the business dropped the moment George died, so we made a counter offer. Since he had experience with the company we pointed him to a banker who indicated that Al could probably qualify for SBA (Small Business Administration) loan programs, as long as he had a decent credit score.

Maybe he was embarrassed, maybe he was just being defiant, but Al didn't bother to tell us that he had a bad credit rating and would not qualify for the SBA loan. Instead he went on a tirade how he helped build the company and he should get it for no down payment and would pay it off over 7 years.

The problem with this arrangement was that Pam needed the sale proceeds to live on. Besides the life insurance, it was all she had to create income. And being at risk while the key employee tried to run the business over the next 7 years was very unappealing to her. So she declined the offer.

The Issue of Salary. We decided that, since Pam had experience in the past with the business, and since the key employee was not going to buy, that we would pay Pam a wage in the meanwhile by making her president of the company; we can only do that, because she had already been listed as an officer (Secretary) of the company, so we just elevated her position to President and continue George's salary to Pam. This will not work in every situation, but Pam was completely justified as she stepped in to keep the company running until another buyer could be found.

The business was operating well with Pam at the helm. The key employee was however, becoming a detriment as he started to spread rumors that, despite his efforts to "save the company", Pam was going to run the company into the ground. What a nightmare. And unfortunately, we had nothing in place to stop him.

Documents that were missing in the overall plan included;

- **Planning Instructions**; things like *Living Trusts* and *Business Continuity Instructions*. Documents that would help us know details and avoid lawyers and court proceedings.

- **Financial Plan**; An analysis of cash flow needs (like *Salary Continuation* and a *Family Income plan* in the event of an emergency) and a plan to make them happen.

- **Business Agreements** like an *Employment Agreement* and a *Stay Bonus* plan between the key employee and the business that would spell out the conditions of employment (no spreading rumors, no discussing trade secrets) and incentives for the employee(s) to stay with the company as it dealt with the aftermath of a disaster.

- **Business Management** documents like *Key Performance Indicators* and *Problem Receivables* checklists would help a new manager come into the business and have a sense of how it's doing and who to keep an eye on.

The combination of these documents and financial instruments (like enough life insurance) would have saved Pam a year of agony. As a matter of fact, if George had $3,000,000 of life insurance (20x his annual income) instead of $1,000,000 (5x his annual income), Pam could have practically given the company to the key employee and saved herself a year of agony as she worked on keeping the business running, getting it ready for sale, and entertaining offers from 3 different buyers.

CHAPTER 6. A PLAN TO PROTECT YOUR FAMILY

From working with business owners for over 30 years, I have learned that there are 3 common "rules" pertaining to planning:

1. Most Business Owners have no time to plan -- they are too busy running the business.

2. They are mostly thinking about growth, not protection of their business or families.

3. They have advisors, but those advisors are primarily engaged to put out fires and they don't tend to talk about things like protecting the business.

With these 3 rules of planning in mind, we developed the 5 Step Family Protection plan, a no-fluff overview with essential planning steps that can be done fairly quickly and inexpensively. These steps can be handled by the business owner or (more likely) delegated to their spouse or even an assistant. Who does these steps (and with whom) is not as important as that they all get done.

TAKE THE 15 DAY CHALLENGE. All of these Planning steps can be underway (and many completed) within a 15 day period. (Remember, ii was 15 days between when Pam said "we should work on the "basics" and when George died suddenly.) Look for the 15 Day Challenge Action Plan at the back of this book.

CHAPTER 7. STEP ONE: AN ESTATE PLAN

Pam had to agonize in hours of meetings with lawyers and accountants to clear the title of the business and business real estate just so she could sell them. An Estate Planning Document called a Living Trust would have saved her the agony of time, because assets would have already been transferred.

Estate planning isn't just for the Ultra-Wealthy, it's a necessary planning need for anyone with a Business or other Real Estate assets. And a Living Trust isn't just a legal document that is full of complex mumbo-jumbo, it's the "family story" that tells what assets exist and where they will go. It's the means for family harmony, by making sure everyone is taken care of properly and fairly, and along with the other documents, commonly a "Pour over Will" (that covers the disposition of special heirloom assets and smaller assets) and a Durable Power of Attorney (that gives permission for other to speak for you if you can't speak for yourself) and Advanced Health Care Directives (that tell doctors and other medical professionals your wishes in the event you can't speak for yourself), creating the Estate planning package is one of the most important uses of your time, should it be needed in the future.

Just ask Pam, she sat through meetings with Accountants and Attorneys just to clear George's name off of the Business, Real Estate and other Assets so she would have the right to sell them.

And here's a thought -- while I don't believe it is as desirable as working with a competent Professional Law firm experienced in Estate and Business matters, even a basic Living Trust and Estate Planning package from an online service like LegalZoom.com that can be done at midnight from your computer for under $500 would have been better than what Pam had, which was nothing.

CHAPTER 8. STEP TWO: BUSINESS CONTINUITY INSTRUCTIONS

Remember the questions that Pam had asked me in the meeting just after George died? The Business Continuity Instructions form answers many of the questions that Pam and others had about George's specific intentions for business management and operations and its employees.

It's kind of like a "Will" for the business. There are also other questions concerning who George might suggest we contact to find a buyer, instead of us having to start from scratch, and who George thinks Pam should Trust as an advisor. Questions about who can sign checks and who is listed as Guarantor on Credit Lines. Which employees might be a "flight risk? Which Vendors might be a "problem receivable" if the owner died, etc.

The form takes less than 30 minutes to complete and it's available on our website. Business continuity instructions are written guidelines for who, how and what you would recommend to handle the management and disposition of the business.

Action Step: Download and complete a Business Continuity form today by clicking on "I Want to Learn How to Protect my Family", then "Business Continuity Instructions" at

www.BeWellPlanned.com

CHAPTER 9. STEP THREE: A FUNDING PLAN

When it comes to providing ready cash at the precise moment it's needed the most (the death of an owner or key employee), nothing beats life insurance. The key is to have an adequate amount life insurance.

Pam received $1 million from a life insurance policy when George died, but $3 million would have been much better. Why? Well, because each $1 million provides about $40,000 of income per year after taxes (assuming a yield before taxes of about 6% and 33% taxes owed), and Pam needed about $120,000 per year to maintain her lifestyle. So $3,000,000 would have provided the $120,000 Pam needed very easily, allowing Pam to breathe easier when it came to her needing to sell the business.

Having more life insurance would have given Pam more options to sell the business faster to the employee or others because she would not be counting on the proceeds to provide income.

And when it comes to the type of life insurance, the most important thing is to have the right amount of death benefit, and often that means buying Term Life insurance for 10, 15 or 20 years. I've never met a beneficiary who cared one bit what type of policy was paying the death benefit, they just want to know one thing – "is it enough to take care of me"?

We've set up a online Insurance Calculator to help business owners or their spouses shop and compare life insurance rates without a life insurance agent. This will give you a chance to figure out what insurance costs are among several companies without having someone breathe down your neck. You can even complete an application online if you want.

Action Step: **Go to the online Insurance Calculator today and plug in your age and presumed insurability status (based on your health profile) and an amount that represents 10 to 30 times your annual income. Start with 10 year term then see what 15 or 20 year term would cost. The Insurance Calculator is located online at** **www.BeWellPlanned.com**

CHAPTER 10. STEP FOUR: AN INCOME PLAN

Pam needed George's paychecks to continue while she sorted things out, unfortunately the IRS won't allow for pay to unqualified individuals. I mentioned earlier that in George and Pam's case, she was already named in the Corporate Records as an Officer (Secretary) of the Corporation, so we were able, with a Corporate Resolution, to make her the President, eligible to receive George's salary.

But if you don't have that situation, you should have something called a **"Salary Continuation Plan"** in the corporate minutes. It's a very simple document that allows for the tax-deductible continuation of the President's (or any other named Executive's) salary to continue as a benefit to the named beneficiary for a period of time.

You see, according to the IRS, a Salary must be "Earned" (they even call it "earned income". Otherwise, the income may be classified as a "Shareholder Dividend" (dividends are distributions of excess profits) which may incur extra taxes (depending on the type of company you have). Also, Dividends are not necessarily payable on a monthly basis and are certainly not a guaranteed source of income. So a strategy to continue income won't take much time to put together, but it must be in place in case of the Death or Disability of the Owner.

While we're on finances, two other critical things should be looked into. First, **who else in the company can sign checks**? If the answer is "no

5 Ways to Protect Your Family | www.BeWellPlanned.com

one" or "I don't know", you should get a plan together so that your spouse or someone else in the business can sign checks. Know now – the time to find out no one else can sign checks is not when the owner dies and payroll is due – very messy.

Also, is there a **Line of Credit** or Business Loan that is being used by your company? Who is listed as the Payer / Guarantor, and what happens if that person dies? In most cases that I have seen, the Owner is the Payer / Guarantor alone (as it was in George's case for the company Line of Credit.) When George died, the Bank they were working with called the Line of Credit immediately after his death. Pam had to jump through a lot of hoops to get it re-opened, just barely in time to make payroll. See if the business owner's spouse can be added to the Credit Line so that it will continue if the business owner dies.

Action Step Checklist:

Get info regarding a Salary Continuation Plan at our website by clicking on **5 steps to protect my business, my family, my employees**, then "**Salary Continuation Instructions**" at

www.BeWellPlanned.com

Find out who else can sign company checks: _____

Will credit lines be called if the Owner dies? ( ) Yes   ( ) No

22 | P a g e

CHAPTER 11. STEP FIVE: A KEY EMPLOYEE STRATEGY

Your key employees are the lifeblood of your company, but they are only human, and at the time of a crisis, they will have some important decisions to make. If you want your key employees to own your company in the event you die, make it easy for them with a **One-Way Buy-Sell plan**. This is a written agreement that states that in the event of your death (and you can also add in a provision in the event of your total disability), they will buy the business from your spouse for a prescribed value (based on an annually updated value or a formula that will be used at the time of death or disability).

In conjunction with the One-Way Buy-Sell, your key employee should be the owner and beneficiary of a life insurance policy on the owner's life for the purchase amount of the business. Here's why: if your key employee is obligated to buy the business from you under the One-Way Buy-Sell agreement when you die, the fastest and easiest way for them to come up with the cash will be for them to have a life insurance policy on you.

They must be the Owner and Beneficiary of the policy (and either pay the premiums themselves or have the business pay the premium and include it in their taxable income) so that they can receive the death proceeds from the policy income tax-free. (If you want to make it "cost neutral" to the employee, provide them with a "double bonus", that is, a bonus for the premium amount and a second bonus to cover the taxes they will owe.)

So, if you die, the key employee receives the insurance proceeds tax-free and pays them to your spouse to purchase the business. Afraid they may be a "flight risk?" No problem, you can appoint a "Trustee" to receive the death proceeds on their behalf to make sure the transaction takes place. And if the business is worth more than the policy, the One-Way Buy-Sell agreement will call for installments to be paid for a period of time (normally 5 years) for the balance to your spouse with interest.

If you are more concerned that your key employee(s) stay with the company instead of buying the business, you can implement a **Stay Bonus** program, along with an **Employment Agreement**, with the goal being to persuade key employees to stay with the company and dissuade them from spreading rumors that might ruin the company.

In our case the key employee couldn't get access to capital to buy the business, and when he found out he wouldn't be the owner, he tried to sabotage the business by spreading rumors. Since there was no employment agreement in place, we had no recourse to stop the rumors.

A Stay Bonus plan coupled with an Employment Agreement would have offered the key employee money for staying with the business during transition as long as he don't disparage the company or leak sensitive information (in which case he would have forfeited the Bonus money.)

Action Step: Go to our Website and click on "I want to learn how to Protect my Family" and read our free report under "Employee Retention", then request a consultation to design a plan. The website is at www.BeWellPlanned.com

CHAPTER 12. THE GOOD NEWS

Let's sum up. We've been talking about the 5 steps to Protect Your Family including;

1. An Estate Plan including a Living Trust.

2. Business Continuity Instructions.

3. Adequate financial funding through life insurance.

4. A Salary Continuation Plan, and;

5. A Key Employee Purchase or Retention Strategy.

Maybe you have one or two of these steps in place, but I will tell you that you need all five of these to have a complete Business Continuity plan.

- The **good news** is that none of the five recommended strategies are very expensive or time- consuming to put in place.

- We've created pages on our website where you can learn about each step and then have resources to implement them inexpensively and quickly.

Visit www.BeWellPlanned.com and take action to take the first step or complete the steps you have not yet taken. We can help you complete your planning quickly, effectively and inexpensively.

In the end, you will be remembered in one of two ways. You will be remembered for your planning, or for your lack of planning. My goal is to make sure that what happened to George and Pam doesn't happen to you and your family.

CHAPTER 13. THE 15 DAY CHALLENGE

Well, you made it to the end. You've met George and Pam and heard all about Pam's horrible, agonizing year of picking up the pieces and getting things in order.

Now it's time to act. I'll lay down the challenge and why I think you should accept it.

The Challenge: Take action starting tomorrow to get all of the 5 steps in motion within the next 15 days.

Why I implore you to do this:

1. George and Pam and I came to the realization that the "basics" weren't done on March 1. 15 days later he died suddenly and the last year has been agony for Pam.

2. All I could think of when I heard he died was "I wish I had a time machine that went back 15 days – we could have got so much done".

3. You love your family = you don't want them to suffer to pick up the pieces of your planning that you could have done easily – and inexpensively – do you?

4. No Living Trust = Time and expense of Lawyers, Probate Court, and several meetings

5. No Business Continuity Instructions = The time and expense of several Meetings with Lawyers and Bankers and CPAs to try and figure out what could have been written down in 30 minutes.

6. Inadequate life insurance = Agonizing time and sale preparation and negotiations to try to squeeze out enough sale proceeds to invest for income when an application form and a blood test could have provided capital inexpensively with a life insurance policy

7. Lack of Income Plan = Financial Planning and Lawyer fees to develop a strategy to provide income for your family with a 3 page document could have been put in the corporate minutes in less than 1 hour.

8. Lack of Key Employee Sale or Retention plan = countless hours combatting your key employee who may try to wreck the value of your company because you did not take 2 hours to design and implement a simple plan to retain, reward and motivate them to help the company.

9. Lack of completing all 5 steps = forcing your spouse, who is shocked and bewildered and only wants to plan for your life celebration and grieve and figure out the rest of her life and help your children, to deal with an overwhelming array of issues and problems.

Start today. Take the 15 day challenge.

Go to www.BeWellplanned.com and start clicking on the areas you want to implement. Each of the 5 areas discussed in this E-book will be found under the tab "I want to Learn **5 steps to protect my business, my family, my employees**".

As you go through each of the 5 steps, you will find that we offer resources to help you implement the steps. It is NOT imperative that you work with us. It IS imperative that you get the 5 steps done.

If you are able to get all 5 steps in motion in 15 days (on the Honor System), email me at BillBlack@ExitCoach.biz**. Tell me "I met the 15 day challenge".**

I promise to mention your business on the Exit Coach Radio Show and promote you as a "Well-Planned Business Owner" with a hyperlink to your business on our website.

Thank you for reading. Thank you for caring. Please tell your Business Owner friends about this material and the other materials at www.BeWellPlanned.com.

We at Exit Coach Radio are here for you, our hero, the private business owner, so that YOU can be well-planned!

ABOUT THE AUTHOR

Bill Black has been helping business owners for over 3 decades to protect and grow their business. Business Owners have always been his heroes, as he came from an entrepreneurial family and has seen the impact that planning can have on Owners and their families in the success and failure of business. Bill is on a quest to help 1 million Business Owners become aware of their need to protect and plan with…

…The Exit Coach Radio Show on KLAA (AM830 in So. California);

…his daily Podcast "The Exit Coach Radio Show", which can be listened to from mobile devices via the "Audio Library" at ExitCoachRadio.com. The podcast is also available via syndication in iTunes, Stitcher and many other mobile platforms;

…his website, ExitCoachRadio.com, which contains numerous "self-serve" resources and planning tools for business owners who want to do basic planning with minimal expense or help from outside advisors;

…monthly Webinars that help business owners and their families learn about concepts and strategies that will help their business (find out about upcoming webinars on the ExitCoachRadio.com site);

…with his books available at www.ExitCoachRadio.com

Help Bill motivate 1,000,000 Business Owners to plan…Share this Book!

www.ingramcontent.com/pod-product-compliance
Lightning Source LLC
Chambersburg PA
CBHW080529190526
45169CB00008B/3109